P9-CLP-398

DISCARD

First Lady

HILLARY RODHAM CLINTON

by Suzanne LeVert

A Gateway Biography
The Millbrook Press
Brookfield, Connecticut

Library of Congress Cataloging-in-Publication Data
LeVert, Suzanne.
Hillary Clinton, first lady / by Suzanne LeVert.
p. cm. — (A Gateway biography)
Includes bibliographical references and index.
ISBN 1-56294-432-0 (lib. bdg.) ISBN 1-56294-726-5 (pbk.)
1. Clinton, Hillary Rodham — Juvenile literature. 2. Clinton,
Bill, 1946– — Juvenile literature. 3. Presidents' wives — United
States — Biography — Juvenile literature. [1. Clinton, Hillary
Rodham. 2. First ladies.] I. Title. II. Series.
E887.C55L48 1994
973.929′092 — dc20 [B] 93-13836 CIP AC

Cover photo courtesy of Wide World Photos
Background cover photo courtesy of Superstock

Photos courtesy of Wide World Photos: pp. 4, 29 (top), 33,
39 (bottom); Sygma: pp. 9, 12 (© Alan Hawes), 20 (John
Ficara), 23, 26, 29 (bottom), 30, 34, 37 (Mike Stewart); UPI/
Bettmann: pp. 11, 17, 39 (top); Reuters/Bettmann: pp. 41, 42.

Published by The Millbrook Press
2 Old New Milford Road
Brookfield, Connecticut 06804

Hillary Rodham Clinton

First Lady Hillary Rodham Clinton talks to reporters about her National Health Care Task Force in April 1993. Listening are senators Bob Dole (left) and George Mitchell.

On *January 25, 1993,* Hillary Rodham Clinton accepted a new job as chairwoman of the National Health Care Task Force. As head of this group, Hillary would lead a panel of experts to find the solution to a serious problem: How to make sure that everyone in the United States received medical care at a reasonable cost.

The job required someone very organized and with an understanding of the economy and the law. It was also important for the person who took on this task to have compassion for the poor and disadvantaged.

Hillary Rodham Clinton met all those requirements. At forty-five years of age, she had been a lawyer for more than twenty years. Much of her work as an attorney had involved defending the interests of private businesses. She had also worked tirelessly for social programs to benefit the public. Twice before, she had tackled complicated issues as head of a governmental task force.

All eyes were focused on Hillary Rodham Clinton when she took on this new job. Although few people questioned her abilities, her appointment was not accepted by everyone. After all, the man who appointed her was not only the president of the United States; he was also her husband, Bill Clinton. Some people felt that it was unfair for an elected official to give political power to a family member. Others stressed that Hillary should devote herself to the regular duties of the First Lady and not take on additional responsibilities.

Hillary, however, accepted the position. Questions about her proper role in her husband's life were not new to her. All her life she had risen to meet the many challenges that face women who are intelligent and ambitious. She knew she could meet this one as well.

Hillary Diane Rodham was born on October 26, 1947, in Park Ridge, Illinois. Her parents, Hugh and Dorothy Rodham, chose to raise their family in this quiet suburb of Chicago for many reasons. Its tree-lined streets were peaceful, and its residents were politically conservative and religious. Most important, its school system was one of the best in the state.

Educating Hillary and her younger brothers, Hugh, Jr., and Tony, was a top priority for Hugh and Dorothy. The owner of a small textile company, Hugh grew up having to struggle to get ahead in life. He wanted his children to have all the opportunities a good education provided.

Hillary received special encouragement from her mother, who was a full-time homemaker. Dorothy believed that her daughter should have many options to choose from when it came time to decide on her future. "Just because she was a girl didn't mean she should be limited," Dorothy later told a reporter.

Hillary loved to learn and excelled at school. But she also loved sports, especially basketball, and other after-school activities. By the time she was ten years old, she could perform on toe shoes in ballet class. She had also earned almost every Girl Scout badge offered. Her brothers, Hugh (who was then seven years old) and Tony (who was three), were her constant playmates. The three Rodham children would always be close friends.

From a young age, Hillary was aware that there were people less fortunate than she and her neighbors in Park Ridge. Hugh once took his children to meet the hardworking but poor men and women who worked in the Pennsylvania coal mines — coal mines where he himself had toiled during the Great Depression of the 1930s. Hugh and Dorothy taught their children that they had a responsibility to help those in need. It was a lesson Hillary never forgot.

Hillary entered Maine East High School in 1962. Her freshman year was an exciting one, not only at school but also at her church. A young and energetic minister named Don Jones was appointed to head the First Methodist Church's youth group. Hillary Rodham was a faithful member of the group.

The Reverend Don Jones involved Hillary and her fellow members in new activities. He took the group on trips into the poorest sections of Chicago. When they visited a recreation center in one of the city's toughest neighborhoods, they met with young people their own age who lived in poverty. Jones also took the group to visit migrant farm workers who lived near Park Ridge. Hillary saw with her own eyes how people without the same

Hillary is shown here with her high school debating team. She was an articulate and forceful speaker.

opportunities she was given often suffered. She vowed to help in any way she could.

With the Reverend Jones's help, she and her friends set up a baby-sitting service to care for the children of the migrant workers. Hillary also organized circuses and amateur sports tournaments to raise money. The funds went to the migrant workers and to help the youth groups in the city. Hillary's generous spirit and sense of humor helped to make these events both fun and successful.

A high point for Hillary came that same year when Jones took Hillary and her group to a church in Chicago where the Reverend Martin Luther King, Jr., was speaking. After the speech, Jones took Hillary and the rest of the youth group backstage to meet the famous civil rights leader. Hillary's eyes shone with admiration for this dedicated and courageous man.

At school, Hillary continued to excel. She enjoyed reading novels and philosophy. She was also challenged by the sciences. She was especially interested in the race between the United States and the Soviet Union to put a man on the moon. When she was a junior in high school, she wrote to the

Hillary was thrilled when she had the chance to hear civil rights leader Martin Luther King, Jr., speak at a church in Chicago.

Hillary poses with other members of the student council. Ambitious and talented, she knew by the time she finished high school that she would study law.

National Aeronautics and Space Administration (NASA) to ask how to become an astronaut. She was furious when NASA wrote back to say that "girls need not apply." (NASA later changed this policy.)

By the time she was a senior, Hillary had a new career goal: to become a lawyer. She had the skills necessary. Not only was she very smart, but she was able to see all sides of an issue. Most important, she could argue passionately for what she believed in and convince others that her position was the right one.

Hillary was also a natural leader. Her fellow students elected her chairwoman of the high school's organization committee, which made her responsible for running the school's assemblies. In June 1965 she graduated from high school in the top five percent of her class. She was also voted the girl most likely to succeed.

Hillary decided to attend Wellesley College, in a suburb of Boston, Massachusetts. Two of her high school teachers had gone to Wellesley, one of the finest women's schools in the country. Although Hillary was a little nervous about leaving home, she was also eager to face the challenges ahead.

Hillary *went to college* during an exciting time in our country's history. The civil rights movement, which urged equality for African Americans and all minorities, inspired students on campuses across the country, including Wellesley. By 1967 college students had joined with other people to oppose the United States government's war in Vietnam, a country in Southeast Asia. Many people thought it was wrong to interfere in the affairs of a country that posed no threat to the United States.

Another political movement that began in the late 1960s was the fight for women's rights. Women wanted the same opportunities for jobs and wages as men had. They demanded the right to make their own decisions about whether to work outside the home or to become full-time homemakers.

All of these issues fueled Hillary's love of politics and the law. She majored in political science and studied hard at school. But, just as she had in high school, Hillary enjoyed other activities too.

Hillary was a pretty young woman with a ready smile. She had fun with her classmates and was popular with the young men she met from nearby colleges. She went to football games and dances. More than anything, she loved getting together with friends to discuss politics.

At the same time, Hillary also kept her commitment to helping those less fortunate than she. During her freshman year, she traveled to Roxbury, a poor section of Boston, to teach young black children to read. Helping children became her primary focus.

Hillary became a leader on campus too. Because she could understand both sides of even the most difficult issues, she was able to form bridges between groups with different goals. During her freshman year, African-American women demanded that more blacks be allowed to enter Wellesley. Hillary worked with the group and the college administration, helping them to communicate with one another.

In her senior year, Hillary was elected president of the college government. As president, she organized the first teach-ins on the Vietnam War to be held at Wellesley. These meetings explained the complicated war to interested students.

In the spring of her senior year, Hillary and her

classmates decided that they wanted to have a student be one of the speakers at the graduation ceremony. Up to that time, students had not been allowed to participate. Hillary negotiated with the administration until the students were given permission. When the women of Wellesley College voted on the best person to represent them as the speaker, Hillary Rodham was chosen.

At that time it was traditional for the administration to invite an outside speaker to graduation. At Hillary's graduation that speaker was Senator Edward Brooke, a liberal Republican from Massachusetts. Brooke delivered his message just before Hillary stood up to begin hers. Hillary felt that the senator had not addressed the most important issues of the day. Instead of simply reading her prepared speech, she began by criticizing Brooke's message. Then she read her own, which urged her fellow graduates to devote their lives to improving society.

Hillary's performance shocked some of the people who attended the graduation. Many others admired her courage and quick thinking. Hillary's words and actions attracted national attention. An

Like Hillary Rodham, the students in this photo made
their feelings on political issues known during graduation.
The student on the left wears a peace symbol and the
students to the right wear black power and peace symbols.

excerpt from her speech — and her picture — was published in *Life* magazine, a fitting end to a brilliant college career.

Hillary left Wellesley and headed for Yale Law School in New Haven, Connecticut. She chose Yale because it stressed public service instead of private business law. Many Yale law graduates went on to work in government. In fact, many of Hillary's professors at Yale had been members of the John F. Kennedy administration in the early 1960s.

Hillary quickly became a leader at Yale. In the spring of 1970 she led a mass meeting of the student body. Students were demanding that Yale Law School become more involved in social issues. They threatened to boycott — to stop going to classes — if their demands were not met. Slowly but surely, Hillary led the protesters and the administration to a solution. The law school would stay open but would also pay more attention to what was going on outside the university.

Hillary's desire to work on behalf of children grew at Yale. When Hillary met Marian Wright

Edelman, a former Yale Law School student, a friendship and partnership began that would last for decades. Edelman had been involved with the rights of children since she graduated from Yale and was impressed with Hillary's commitment. She helped the eager young student find the best courses and programs to spur her interest.

During her first two years in law school, Hillary took several courses on the law as it related to children. Then she was accepted in a special program at Yale's Child Study Center. There, she helped to research a book called *Beyond the Best Interests of the Child,* published in 1973. This book was about how the legal system should treat children of divorced parents and children who are physically abused.

Hillary also assisted the Child Study Center's nursery school teachers and learned as much as she could about how children learn and grow. She impressed her instructors with her understanding of children and their needs. Her compassion for young people grew deeper when she started to work directly with abused children at the Yale–New Haven Hospital.

Marian Wright Edelman became Hillary's good friend and mentor. They shared a deep-seated interest in defending the rights of children.

With Marian Wright Edelman's help, Hillary was made a member of the Carnegie Council on Children. As a member, she wrote a number of papers on children's legal rights. Of special concern to her were a child's right to go to school and to receive good medical treatment.

Although Hillary worked hard, she also had an active social life. Many of the people she met at Yale remained lifelong friends, like Edelman. Indeed, Hillary met one of the most important people in her life one day while passing through the student center at Yale.

"And not only that, we grow the biggest watermelons in the world," she heard a booming male voice with a southern accent say. When she asked a friend who this young man was, she was told that his name was Bill Clinton. Hillary wanted to know more about this good-looking, friendly man.

Bill Clinton came from Arkansas and was one of the southern state's biggest fans. He had graduated from Georgetown University in Washington, D.C., then gone to study at Oxford in England on a Rhodes scholarship. He was at Yale to receive a law degree but did not intend to practice law. Instead, his ambition was to go into politics. He wanted to be elected to public office in Arkansas so that he could help the people of his home state.

Just as Hillary had noticed Bill, Bill was also aware of the charming and intelligent Hillary Rodham. One day Hillary noticed Bill staring at her from across the room at the law school library. In her usual direct way, she walked right up to him and introduced herself.

Once they started talking, they found out how much they had in common. They were both dedicated to improving life for the poor, especially women and children. And they both loved politics. In 1972, Hillary and Bill took time off from law school to work together on the presidential campaign of Democrat George McGovern.

In some ways, though, Hillary and Bill were opposites. Hillary tended to be quiet and serious. Bill was outgoing and full of fun. Hillary had decided that she wanted to live and work in a big city. Bill, on the other hand, was committed to returning to the rural state of Arkansas. Although the two were in love, they decided to go their separate ways after graduating from law school. Bill went

Hillary Rodham and Bill Clinton.

south to Arkansas, while Hillary moved north to Massachusetts.

When *Hillary graduated* from law school in 1973, her impressive grades and work experience brought many job offers. She decided to join the Children's Defense Fund, an organization founded by her friend Marian Wright Edelman. Then located in Cambridge, Massachusetts, the Fund helped poor children and families find the resources they needed to get ahead in life. Hillary worked there for about six months.

Then, in January 1974, Hillary was offered a unique opportunity. The House Judiciary Committee in Washington, D.C., was investigating President Richard Nixon in what was known as the Watergate scandal. Hillary's task was to set forth the proper legal process for an investigation into his supposed illegal activities. Once again, she was able to look at a controversial issue with objectivity.

When Nixon resigned as president on August 9, 1974, because of the scandal, Hillary was out of a job. Although many Washington law firms wanted to hire her, she made a surprising decision. She chose to take a job at a law school in Arkansas so that she could be with Bill Clinton.

Just before Hillary arrived in Arkansas, Bill, a Democrat, made an important decision of his own. He would make his first run for public office: a seat in Congress then held by a Republican, John Hammerschmidt. He was thrilled when Hillary Rodham agreed to be his campaign manager.

In fact, the whole Rodham family — Hillary's parents and her two brothers, Hugh and Tony — took an apartment in Fayetteville, Arkansas, so that they could give Bill Clinton a hand with the campaign. The Rodham family would stay close to Bill and Hillary in the years to come.

Although Bill lost the election, Hillary's respect for his commitment and ambition grew deeper. The two people fell deeper in love, too. In 1975, Bill asked Hillary to marry him. She said yes. A partnership based on love and respect began in earnest.

A year later, Hillary found herself packing up and moving from the pleasant town of Fayetteville. Bill Clinton had won the election to become state attorney general, and his new office was located in

Hillary decided to move to Arkansas to be with Bill. From the start, her role in his political career was unusually vital.

26

Little Rock, the Arkansas capital. Hillary's career also received a boost when she was asked to join a prestigious Little Rock law practice called the Rose Law Firm. As a member of the firm, Hillary concentrated largely on business and corporate law.

Her dedication to the needs of children did not end, though. In 1976 she helped to found the nonprofit Arkansas Advocates for Children and Families. This group of attorneys tried to identify the problems facing poor children in the state and then find solutions. This was a cause close to Hillary's heart. At the same time, Hillary began to try criminal cases with a new friend and associate, William R. Wilson. Wilson admired Hillary's legal skills and observed that she had a unique ability to "appeal to your mind and your heart at the same time."

In 1978, Hillary's life changed dramatically when Bill Clinton became the youngest governor in the history of Arkansas. Clinton promised to work hard to improve education and health care for the poor people of his state.

When Hillary became First Lady of Arkansas, people began to look more closely at her. Some of them were disturbed that she had chosen to keep her own last name, Rodham, rather than take her husband's. Others thought she should give up her career to fulfill the duties of First Lady. Hillary refused, saying, "I need my own identity, too."

Bill Clinton's first term as governor provided Hillary with a unique opportunity. Bill appointed her to head a task force called the Rural Health Advisory Committee. As chairwoman, Hillary helped to create a program to deliver health care to people in small, isolated areas of the state.

Both Bill and Hillary were extremely busy with their careers during this exciting time. But they also wanted very much to have a child. And on February 27, 1980, they did, when Hillary gave birth to a daughter, Chelsea Victoria Clinton. Chelsea was named for one of her parents' favorite songs, "Chelsea Morning," sung by Judy Collins. Even though Hillary continued to work outside the home, she vowed to always put her daughter ahead of her personal ambitions.

In 1980, Bill Clinton lost his bid to be reelected governor. The people of Arkansas were upset that his reforms often led to higher taxes or raised fees on such necessities as car licenses. In addition,

Above: Bill was thirty-two years old when he became governor of Arkansas, and Hillary was thirty-one. Right: Hillary with First Lady Rosalynn Carter during her 1979 trip to Arkansas.

Hillary with her two-year-old daughter, Chelsea.

many voters did not feel that Hillary made a good First Lady. She did not pay much attention to fashion, she worked outside the home, and she still used her own last name instead of her husband's.

Hillary was offended by their criticisms. She knew that such things should not matter to anyone but her and her family. But she knew that being in politics to help the people of Arkansas was Bill's dream — and hers too. Both she and Bill thought hard about what they could change. During this period their marriage was strained, but they stayed together.

When Bill decided to make another run for governor in 1982, Hillary made a decision of her own. She would give up using her own last name and go by the name Hillary Rodham Clinton. She felt that if her name kept people from seeing the good her husband and she could do, she would gladly give it up.

It made a difference. Along with Bill Clinton's promise to listen more carefully to the people of Arkansas before creating new programs, Hillary's name change helped Bill win the governorship in November 1982.

Once again, Governor Clinton tried to improve the educational system in Arkansas. Knowing that someone with integrity and good organizational skills was needed to head the project, he turned to the person he called "the smartest woman I know," Hillary Rodham Clinton.

Hillary worked hard as chairwoman of the Education Standards Committee. She traveled from town to town listening to teachers, students, and parents. In 1983 she issued a report calling for tests to make sure that teachers knew enough to teach. It also recommended that the number of students in every class be made fewer and that the school year be made longer. Hillary and her committee received praise from all over the state.

In addition to working with her husband throughout his many terms as governor, Hillary remained active as one of the chief partners in the Rose Law Firm. She joined several corporate boards. She also received national attention when she was named one of the "100 Most Influential Lawyers in America" by the *National Law Journal* in 1988. (The honor was bestowed on Hillary a second time, in 1991.)

Hillary and Bill celebrate his victory in the Democratic race for governor in 1982. Bill was reelected, and Hillary became the head of his educational reform project.

Hillary and Bill in 1983. During Bill's second term in office, the people of Arkansas stood behind the dynamic young couple's efforts to improve the state. Bill would serve for three more terms as governor.

Meanwhile, Governor Clinton was often in the national spotlight as well. In 1988 he gave the speech nominating Michael Dukakis for president at the Democratic National Convention. A year later President George Bush asked him to be co-chairman of a national meeting of governors. In 1990, Bill Clinton was named chairman of the Democratic Leadership Council, a group of mostly southern party leaders. As he traveled throughout the country, Bill began thinking about running for president of the United States.

That same year Bill almost decided not to make a run for a fifth term as governor. Hillary called up a friend who was a former newspaper publisher in Arkansas, and asked, "What would happen if *I* ran for governor?" Her friend told her that she might well have a chance to win. Although Hillary decided not to run and Bill was reelected, some people thought Hillary Rodham Clinton would make an even better governor than her husband.

In the fall of 1991, Hillary wrote in a letter to a good friend: "We are about to start a great adventure." With Hillary's full support, Bill Clinton had decided to run for president of the United States. Hillary took a leave of absence from her law firm to join in the campaign.

As usual, Hillary's number one concern was her daughter, Chelsea. She worried about how the eleven-year-old girl would be affected by the campaign. She and Bill decided that Chelsea would live with Hillary's parents, Hugh and Dorothy, who had moved to Little Rock in 1987. That way, Chelsea could stay in her regular school when her parents were away. Most important, Hillary and Bill wanted to keep Chelsea away from the spotlight of the media.

In January 1992 the Clinton campaign was upset by a shocking newspaper story. A woman named Gennifer Flowers claimed that she once had a love affair with Bill Clinton while he was married to Hillary. The scandal rocked the campaign, but Hillary stood by her husband. She admitted that their marriage had not been perfect, but she stressed her love and respect for Bill Clinton.

Despite the grace Hillary displayed, public opinion of her dropped. At the same time, some of

Hillary and Chelsea look on as Bill announces he will be a candidate.

the candidates running against Bill began to strike out at Hillary Rodham Clinton. In particular, Republican president George Bush's campaign accused Hillary of not believing that family life was as important as a career or politics.

Hillary's image as a tough career woman would remain an issue throughout the campaign. In March 1992 a reporter asked her a question about her law practice. She replied, "I suppose I could have stayed home and baked cookies and had teas." Millions of women who had never worked outside the home read Hillary's statement as an insult.

Finally, Hillary decided to show the American people how important her family was to her. For the first time, she allowed Chelsea to be interviewed and photographs of herself and Chelsea to be published. She went out of her way to praise women who chose to stay home to raise families. Although she remained active behind the scenes, she made fewer political speeches than she had at the start of the campaign.

In the end, Bill Clinton pulled ahead of George Bush to win the election. Hillary Rodham Clinton

July 17, 1992: Bill and Hillary share a relaxed moment before a campaign speech with Al Gore, Bill's vice presidential running mate, and his wife, Tipper. Hillary and Tipper were old friends.

Sept 30, 1992: Hillary was in the spotlight during much of Bill's campaign. Here, she speaks to a crowd in Rhode Island.

became First Lady of the United States on January 20, 1993. Millions of Americans were excited to see what kind of First Lady this strong and independent woman would be. They knew she would make a good role model for young girls and families across the country.

Five days later her husband appointed her to head the National Health Care Task Force. She immediately set to work in her new office in the West Wing of the White House, just a floor above her husband's office.

Sadly, her father Hugh Rodham, who was eighty-one years old, suffered a stroke on March 19, 1993, in Little Rock, Arkansas. Hillary canceled her appointments and went immediately to his bedside. He died several weeks later, on April 7.

Although Hillary was greatly saddened by his death, she soon returned to Washington ready to lead her task force. She devoted herself to the difficult job of creating a solid plan to reform health care for the American people.

At the same time, she, Bill, and Chelsea adjusted to their new lives in the White House. Despite their hectic schedules, the family meets every

*November 3, 1992: The victory celebration at the
Old Statehouse in Little Rock, Arkansas.*

As First Lady, Hillary continues to view the future of America's children as her primary concern.

night for dinner, and both Hillary and Bill help Chelsea with her homework. "We lead a life that in many ways is like the lives of other people who are working and raising families," Hillary told a reporter, "but obviously it is very different, too." No doubt Hillary Rodham Clinton will face the challenges of juggling a high-profile career and family life with characteristic energy and commitment.

Important Dates

1947   Hillary Diane Rodham is born on October 26 in Park Ridge, Illinois.

1969   Graduates from Wellesley College, Massachusetts.

1973   Graduates from Yale Law School, New Haven, Connecticut.

1974   Accepts a teaching position at the University of Arkansas School of Law.
        Marries Bill Clinton.

1976   Joins the Rose Law Firm.

1978   Becomes First Lady of Arkansas.

1979   Accepts an appointment as chairwoman of the Rural Health Advisory Committee.

1980   Gives birth to a daughter, Chelsea Victoria.
        Becomes a partner in the Rose Law Firm.
        Bill Clinton loses the governorship of Arkansas.

1983   Enters the governor's mansion as First Lady a second time.

1983   Heads the Education Standards Committee.

1988   Is named one of the "100 Most Influential Lawyers in the United States of America" by the *National Law Journal.* (Is named again in 1991.)

1991   Joins her husband Bill's campaign for president of the United States.

1993   Becomes First Lady of the United States.
        Accepts the appointment to head the National Health Care Task Force.

Further Reading

Here are some other books about First Ladies that you might enjoy:

Barbara Bush: First Lady of Literacy, by June Behrens (Childrens Press, 1990).

Edith Wilson: The Woman Who Ran the United States, by James C. Giblin (Viking, 1992).

Eleanor Roosevelt: First Lady of the World, by Doris Faber (Viking, 1985).

Mary Todd Lincoln: President's Wife, by LaVere Anderson (Chelsea House Publishers, 1991).

Index

Park Ridge, Illinois, 6
President's National
    Health Care Task
    Force, *4*, 5–6, 40

Rodham, Dorothy, 6–8,
    36
Rodham, Hugh, 6–8, 36,
    40
Rodham, Hugh, Jr., 7,
    25
Rodham, Tony, 7, 25
Rose Law Firm, 27, 32

Rural Health Advisory
    Committee, Arkansas, 28

Vietnam war, 14, 15

Watergate scandal, 24
Wellesley College,
    13–16
Wilson, William R., 27
Women's rights
    movement, 14

Yale Law School, 18–19